Babies Don't Bark

Preparing The Family Dog For The New

Baby

Mike Deathe CPDT-KA

Published by FastPencil Publishing

Babies Don't Bark

First Edition

Print edition ISBN: 978149530891

Copyright © K.I.S.S. Pet Solutions LLC 2021

All rights reserved. No part of this publication may be reproduced, stored in a retrieval system, or transmitted, in any form, or by any means, electronic, mechanical, photocopying, recording, or otherwise, without the prior consent of the publisher.

Sale of this book without a front cover may be unauthorized. If the book is coverless, it may have been reported to the publisher as "unsold or destroyed" and neither the author nor the publisher may have received payment for it.

This book is for informational purposes only. If you have any concerns with your dog with anything having to do with babies or your pregnancy. Contact a dog training professional immediately.

http://www.fastpencil.com

Printed in the United States of America

Table of Contents

Who Am I, And What Do I Know About This Topic? 7
Situation, Time Frame And Expectations 9
Practice With A Doll 11
New Baby Smells 13
New Baby Sounds 15
A Word On Counter Conditioning 17
All That Baby Stuff 19
The Nursery 21
Who's Your Baby? 25
Beds And Couches 27
Skills To Learn; Behaviors To Curb 29
Bringing Baby Home 33
The Gift Of Time 35
The First Introduction! 37
Sniff And Say Hello 39
Management Devices 41
The Big 3 Management Devices 43
Common Issues With Dog And Baby Interactions 47
Dog-Baby Interaction: A Road Map 49
How Age Can Affect Behavior 51
Body Language And More To Consider 53
Dog Bite Statistics And The Anatomy Of A Dog Bite: 55

A Final Thought 57
Afterward 59

Who Am I, And What Do I Know About This Topic?

Hi, I'm Mike. Since May 2016 I have taught a monthly class at a local hospital called *Babies Don't Bark*. The class is designed to get expectant families ready to bring their new two-legged kid home to meet the four-legged ones you already have!

I have two sons, 20 and 17, who both came home to two very large pooches and have been raised around lots of dogs ever since.

I've been a professional dog trainer for the last 12 years. My certification is CPDT-KA (Certified Professional Dog Trainer, Knowledge Assessed). I am also a Canine Good Citizen Evaluator for the American Kennel Club.

So, what does all this mean for you? It means that I know a lot about dogs, I make my living from teaching people how to understand and relate to their dogs, and I have two grown kids who survived the process. Here's the book on what I've learned!

Teaching this subject is a passion of mine. It is simple to do, but will require practice, consistency and frequency on your part to be ready.

Situation, Time Frame And Expectations

Ask yourself the following:

1. How long until the baby arrives?

The more time you have, the more you can practice! There are lots of things you can do to get the family pooch(es) ready for the new arrival. Start using these techniques by the end of the first trimester or beginning of the second. Even if you have less time, people with dogs have been having babies for eons without my class or this book. That said, the more time we have the better: There is a lot for Fido to get used to before the baby comes home.

2. How many dogs do you have?

This is an important question regarding how hard your upcoming transition will be. As I like to remind my clients,

- One dog is a lot of work.
- Two dogs is 3x as much work.
- Three dogs is 9x as much work.
- Four dogs is 81x as much work.

The work grows exponentially with each dog due to the amount of distraction, interpersonal relationships and the sheer amount of time required to do things like feed, take outside, manage personalities and everything else that goes into being a dog owner. Don't panic: My sons were born into a house with two really big dogs (a Malamute and a Great Pyrenees), and they grew up in a 4-dog household!

They each eventually got dogs of their own, plus my two, and the number four just seemed to stick from that point. It can be done, but the more dogs you have, the more prep work you have to do to get the household ready for a new baby.

3. Is this your first child?

If you already have kids, you have some sense of the sleep deprivation, distraction, chaos and the complete change of routine that is about to become your life. If not, you may be blissfully unaware of what is coming! You may not think it will not be all that different from the life you and your dog(s) have now.

However, life is about to change...

Things that you thought were important will fall to the wayside, and things that you never imagined would be important will become critical.

Parenthood is something I cherish above all else. Slow down and enjoy the chaotic ride because before you know it, it will be gone. As far as getting the family dog ready... Let's go over everything we can do to prepare!

Practice With A Doll

As goofy as it sounds your first assignment is to purchase a cloth baby doll, approximately the size of a newborn baby. This is the most direct way to teach Fido how to behave around his or her new baby sibling. The doll will be used several ways to simulate the changes in your body position; carrying a baby alters everything your dog is familiar with.

- How you walk. After all, you are now constantly carrying something new.
- Bending over. You now have a baby that you certainly don't want to drop, so you bend over only to one side, keeping the baby on your hip.
- Picking stuff up off the floor. Again, having to shift weight and bend sideways so as to not fall down or drop the kid. ☺
- Going to the bathroom... A whole new procedure! What do I do with the baby, and what do I do with the dog?
- Cooking dinner. Try to imagine that with both a dog and a child!

The goal here is twofold:

1. Getting yourself in the habit of having a child with you and forcing you to think about how regular household activities are going to change.
2. Letting the dog adjust to the changes, which can take time.

New Baby Smells

A dog's nose has up to 300 million scent receptors, while we humans have only about 6 million. We see and understand our world primarily with our eyeballs, and dogs with their noses. We must figure out the best way to get Fido used to all the new smells that are going to be coming along with their new baby brother or sister. Again, we turn to the baby doll. About once a week (depending on how much time you have before the baby arrives), I want you to introduce a new smell by literally putting it on the baby doll and continuing the usual routine with the baby doll, only now stinky with new smells. Here are some smells to consider and use:

- Baby oil
- Baby powder
- Baby wash
- Baby shampoo
- Baby food
- Diaper wipes
- Diaper rash ointment
- A and D ointment

These are probably not normal smells to your dog right now, and they will definitely be a distraction! As we practice our everyday routines, having added the new body posture changes and now the new smells, we can go a long way to getting the dog used to these things before the baby comes home.

New Baby Sounds

The unique sound of a human baby cry is one that can really puzzle a dog. A crying baby is nothing more than an animal in distress, and this might excite, concern or even agitate a dog. Each dog is different, and the only way to know how your dog is going to react is to allow them to experience the sound.

As with all the techniques in this book, it is strongly recommended that you do this well before the real baby arrives. For one, we can see if there is a major issue to deal with; secondly, so that we can normalize this noise for the dog.

If you Google "crying baby noises for dogs" you will return about one and a half million results, and quite a few of them are MP4's or YouTube videos of minutes and minutes of wailing babies.

We already have the doll, we are carrying it around, and it smells funny… The only thing we are missing is baby sounds! Download an audio file or press play on a video, on your phone and put the phone in the baby doll's clothing or blanket, and we now have a smelly, crying baby doll. We are now one step closer to conditioning your dog to life with a new baby.

You could even use that fancy flat-screen smart TV with the YouTube app so that you could run the audio through your surround sound speakers for a more realistic noise. During this you could practice positive things like hand feeding to create a happy association with the noise.

A Word On Counter Conditioning

We are trying to normalize or "counter condition" the family dog with the sights, smells and sounds of a new baby. The easiest way to do this is to pair the presence of these things with something positive and fun! In most cases the easiest way to do this is with food, but don't just limit yourself to treats. You can pair the new baby simulation with walks, car rides or their favorite toy. Just remember that the goal is also to teach calmness around the baby, so getting the dog all riled up is not something we want to do.

Sometimes when we intend to counter condition a dog, we end up *flooding the dog instead:* Adding too much stimuli for the dog to handle all at once. Flooding may result in a negative behavior: Over excitement, anxiety or even aggression. It is therefore important that these techniques with the baby doll have three main components:

- **High frequency** (*practice every day*)
- **Short duration** (*10-15 minutes each session only*)
- **Under threshold** (*the dog must remain calm*)

Not getting all three may result in the dog learning the exact opposite of what you are trying to teach him or her. Hire a *professional dog trainer if you see anything that makes you uncomfortable. Dog trainers have seen most of these behaviors before and will be able to help you get back on track before the baby comes home; this is wiser than calling us after something bad has happened. Here is another way of looking at it...*

Dog Trainer Tip

If you are including the word "hope" in your thoughts concerning your dog and your new baby (I hope the dog behaves well around the new baby... I hope everything works out...) then you are in over your head and need help! It does not mean something bad will happen, it just means you are not quite as prepared as you might have thought you were. Get help and let's figure this out before the baby comes home.

All That Baby Stuff

Is the nursery completed and ready for the baby's arrival? Or do you, like most expectant parents, have a room completely filled with boxes of unopened baby stuff, equipment and family hand-me-downs that you keep telling yourself you will get to? (No judgments!)

Let's talk about *neophobia: The fear of anything new. Most wild animals are naturally neophobic for survival reasons; those that are fearless of new/novel things don't last long in the wild! Dogs are simply freaked out by stuff they are not used to or have no experience with.*

Ask yourself how your dog will react to a...

- *Johnny jumper*
- *Car seat*
- *Boppy pillow*
- *Highchair*
- *Pack and play*
- *Crib*
- *Play pen*
- *Baby blankets with hanging play items*

- *Mamaroo (that thing moves in all sorts of directions and has a white noise machine built in)*
- *Breast pump*

This list could go on forever, but the poor dog doesn't stand a chance to get used to these things if they are still in boxes! Once unpacked and organized, you can put the smelly, noisy "baby" in and around these items for the dog to see, sniff and get used to (in an at least somewhat realistic scenario).

The Nursery

The Nursery
We have covered the equipment in the room, but what about the room itself? This is going to be the room where the baby sleeps*, gets dressed, nurses and gets diaper changes. Should the dog be allowed in the nursery? First, let me ask you this:

Would you ever leave a baby alone in the bathtub?

Of course, you would not, and that guttural response you had to just reading the question is exactly what I was going for. Now here is a second question:

Would you ever leave a baby and a dog alone together?

If you had the same staunch response of NO to this question, you passed! If not, don't worry I am going to explain, but the short answer is in the word alone.

Dogs do not do well in isolation. In fact, isolation around a problem usually makes the problem worse. If I have a dog who is fearful, reactive or even aggressive around kids and then isolate the dog from the kids, that behavior is likely going to get worse. With professional, supervised counter-conditioning (short duration, high frequency, under thresh-

old training) we can see marked improvement in this type of behavior.

What does any of this have to do with the nursery or the word alone? The dog must get used to the nursery with you present, but never alone. For now, you need to come up with a way to simulate the time you will be spending in the nursery with the dog present and calm, and that is going to take practice. But before practicing you need to have a workable nursery, so getting everything unpacked set up and in its proper home is first priority.

So now that the nursery is set up, the crib is in place, the diaper changing station is ready and you have a chair or place where feeding/nursing will take place, every day you need to go in with your baby doll and the dog and simply sit in the chair. You might have the crying, smelly baby doll in the crib, or maybe with you in the chair. You might even pretend to change a diaper! Heck, this could become your morning location to enjoy your coffee or tea and check emails on your tablet. The point is to get the dog used to just chilling in the room with you. A great idea would be to bring in a dog bed, so they have their own comfy spot to be part of the process. Just remember that **if you leave the room, so does the dog**. We never leave kids and dogs alone!

What if the dog is overexcited or crazy in the nursery? We may want to set up a baby or dog gate and start with the dog being outside the room (but they can see you, so no isolation) until they are calm. Then we can slowly let them into the room. This also gives you a way of only having the dog in the nursery when you are there and keeping the dog out when you are gone.

I hope you are now seeing some of the benefits of the baby doll and being able to practice with and see the issues that might crop up vs. waiting and just hoping it works out with the real baby!

*Unless you are going to be using a bassinet; more on that later.

Who's Your Baby?

Do you consider your dog to be your baby right now? Is your dog the center of your universe? Many of you will answer this question with a resounding YES! *and that is great; however, it is also something we must address now.*

For those first-time parents reading this book, you may not have a realistic idea of what is about to happen to your time and energy; the amount of sleep that will be interrupted and the sheer number of things that will be added to your daily routine by adding a baby to the family. Who do you think is going to receive less attention? Whose walks will decrease in frequency and duration, and who will no longer get to snuggle by you on the couch every night? Let's face it... Your dog's routine is about to get turned upside down.

Now for the choice. Do you want to change that routine now, or wait until the baby gets home? If you wait, who will the dog associate all of these changes with? If you wait until the baby comes home, the changes will be associated with your baby. If you do it now, the changes will be associated with you. Which is the lesser evil?

One sneaky way to reduce your time with your pooch and letting him have fun might be doggy daycare. They get to play with their friends, and you start limiting the amount of time you are actively spending with your dog. Keep in mind not all dogs do well with doggy daycare, so make sure to find a location that is more interested in how your dog is doing than the money you are spending there. Ask your vet or trainer which places they love.

You do not want any negative changes in your dog's life to be associated with your new child.

If you get the changes going now not only do you avoid that issue, but you have a longer period to get the dog used to the new changes.It may be difficult to start taking attention away from the dog now, but better to get him or her used to it rather than wait and hope everything will be alright.

BEDS AND COUCHES

Remember how a crying baby sounds like an animal in distress, and how we can never really predict how a dog will react to that noise? We have smeared all sorts of smelly stuff on a baby doll and practiced, downloaded crying baby noises and practiced some more. We also talked about sleep deprivation and the massive changes everyone, including the dog, will be dealing with.

Now let's talk about bassinets. If your dog is used to sleeping in your bed and you plan on putting a bassinet right next to your bed... Couldn't the dog get into that bassinet? Is there a chance you might be exhausted, and be a heavier sleeper than normal? Does this sound a bit like... Hope? *Now is the time to get a baby gate and get Fido used to sleeping right outside your bedroom door. He or she can come right back into the bedroom once the baby goes into their permanent room.*

For families who will be going straight to the nursery with the baby, the baby gate will be necessary at the nursery door, and the dog can continue to sleep in your room. If you are concerned with a dog being able to jump over the gate* start this process early and test the routine before the baby gets home- this will allow you the time to hire a professional if you see gate-jumping as an issue. All dogs and situations are different!

Couches are a different scenario; I am most concerned with dogs who are used to being on the couches, and not very polite with having to get on or off. There are going to be times when an infant will be on a couch with the parent; the dog might jump on or off the couch a little too enthusiastically and accidentally step on the child. Infant skin is tender and will not hold up well to a dog's feet or nails. Are you hoping nothing bad will happen? Better to change the routine so that the dog cannot get on the couch for a while. Better yet, your nightly practice could involve having the baby doll in a blanket on the couch while the dog is on the couch, to observe his or her behavior.

* Keep in mind that gates come in all different heights now.

Skills To Learn; Behaviors To Curb

"What should my dog know how to do before the baby comes home?"

Knowing how to do a command and being able to do them are completely different. If your dog is reliable* in all of the following skills, you should be on track:

- **Stay**. This command needs to be reliable for duration, distance, and distraction (able to do with all sorts of stuff going on around).
- **Sit**. I use Sit as a way for my dog to request things or say please.
- **Down**. I use Down as my main position when using the Stay command... Dogs tend to be more relaxed in a Down vs. Sit, and this leads to more reliable Stays.
- **Watch me** (or "Look at me"). This is a great redirection command. A dog looking at you and waiting for the next command is not doing anything wrong (Bonus: This one may come in handy with your kids down the road as well!).
- **Leave it.** (Before it's in the mouth).
- **Drop it.** (After it's in the mouth).

- **Recall/Come** when called (Needs to work amidst distraction).
- **Leash skills**. Dog must be able to walk without pulling and follow other commands while on leash.

If you are looking for more specific How To help with these techniques try looking up our YouTube Channel (Mike Deathe with KISS Dog Training) and you will find all sorts of examples and games to play to help with teaching.

Here are some behaviors we must curb before the baby gets home:

- **Jumping up**. This one can be dangerous, but all the work with the baby doll should alert you if this is a problem.
- **Barking**... At the doorbell, out the windows, for attention or just being sassy. This could become an issue with a newborn and sleep schedules. This is mostly an energy/boredom behavior: A bored dog or one with too much pent-up energy will be more likely to speak up! Is your dog getting enough exercise or being mentally stimulated enough?
- **Nippy or snarky** with hands, particularly around food. This one should be obvious and should only be tackled with the help of a professional.
- **Stealing**. There are going to be so many new things that your dog has the opportunity to steal and if this is already a learned behavior, chaos may ensue. Guarding behavior can be a trait of this also; it is urgent to fix it *now. Dogs who have been taught to "trade" items and have not just had things taken away never learn guarding. Teaching a reliable trade command becomes the first step to solving this one.*

- *Trading is the idea of saying to your dog, "You can't have this, but take this other item in exchange." This way the dog never learns to covet or guard items because there is always a fair-trade value. Keep in mind that just because you can safely take something away from a dog does not mean that another family member can do it, and certainly does not mean a child or toddler will be able to. It's much safer to teach a dog that occasionally they will have to give some things up, but there will always be fair and equitable value to replace it.*

There is a lot to teach and un-teach, but the easiest way to audit you and your dog's skills is to take a beginner's class with a reputable trainer. Being in a room with 5 to 7 other dogs and 10 to 12 other people will most definitely highlight the holes in your training!

You could even bring the baby doll to class for a more realistic experience, but I do recommend giving your trainer a heads up before just showing up with a fake infant.

*By reliable I mean able to do these skills in distracting environments (like the outdoors) and with few if any treats.

Bringing Baby Home

Where is your dog going to be while you are in the hospital?

At home with someone staying or checking on them? Going to someone else's home to be watched? Boarding at the local kennel or doggy daycare? You need to know this before you have to head to the hospital. (More on this later).

Is your stuff *and the dog's stuff packed and ready to go?*

Do you have your bags packed? Is the dog's stuff packed and ready to go? Plan and be ready but if you have not thought about this, how can you expect it to go well?

How long will you be at the hospital?

You are probably thinking, "how am I supposed to know?" and that is exactly why I am asking.
It is important to consider how many days you will be in the hospital if you are having a natural childbirth, and how many days if you have a C-section... Both of my boys were born via C-section and neither procedure was planned. Have you talked to your doctor about the amount of time you might spend in the hospital for various versions of childbirth? Be prepared and to be ready for all possibilities.

Dog Trainer Tip

If you have time, having someone bring home socks, beanies or receiving blankets with the baby's scent on it for the dog to smell is an awesome idea. Some hospitals today release moms after just one or two days, but if you can pull it off, GREAT IDEA!

How much time are Mom and Dad taking off?

In many cases moms can take several months off when the baby comes home. Dads are a bit more variable with the amount of time off, typically from a week to several months. Make sure to have all the introductions and routines set before someone has to go back to work, leaving the other one at home with the baby and the dog.

You might have someone in the family on standby to help, or even a doggy daycare or kennel set up to help alleviate pressure if necessary, but don't just hope a family member will be available or that the kennel will have space. Plan now in order to be successful.

The Gift Of Time

In my class, the most popular idea is to have the family dog stay at home and have someone check in on them while the humans are in the hospital, or actually stay at their house with the dog. However, I suggest taking the dog to someone else's home or to a kennel or daycare while you are in the hospital.

This allows you to have a couple of days of peace and quiet without your beloved pet to get the routine with your newborn down! No matter how you prepare or how you think you have things set up, changes to the plan are inevitable.

Also, if you are a first-time parent or especially the parent of the first grandchild in the family, you are going to have tons of people in and out of the house for those first couple of days. Ask yourself; do you really want to try to deal with all of that *and introduce the family dog to the baby on the first day back from the hospital? Sometimes I even use doggy daycare for half days for the first week or so, to make things easier on everyone. Give yourself some grace for a few days to get comfortable before doing the initial introductions.*

The First Introduction!

Pick a day when you have plenty of time to dedicate to the process and at least two people available to do the introductions: One to handle the dog and the other to hold the baby. The introduction will happen on leash so there is more control, and so you can judge the dog's energy level.

One parent will sit on the couch or in a chair, and the other parent or someone else (whom the dog knows and will listen to) will enter the room with the dog on leash. The dog must be calm. If he or she is pulling on the leash or lunging, stop the introduction, leave the room and let the dog calm down before trying again.

This is the moment when the dog's ability to work on-leash calmly and without pulling matters most. A dog who cannot walk nicely on a leash will no doubt have issues in the home as well. If you have a dog like this, get a trainer's help ASAP so that when we start with introductions, we have things going in the right direction. Check out my book called "Whoa Dog Whoa" that specifically covers how to teach loose-leash walking.

Dog Trainer Tip

If you have been smart, this introduction that I am describing will have been done *tons of times already with our* *little buddy the baby doll. Thus, the dog will be already used to and ready for real introduction!*

Once the dog is calm, enter the room again, and this time ask the dog for some basic commands: A Sit, a Down, a couple of Watch Me's... If the dog can pay attention to you then proceed with the introduction but if not, leave the room, get the dog under better control and try again.

It's simple: **Until the dog is calm and listening, do not introduce the dog and the baby**. But as the tip above mentions, you should have this down due to all of the practice that you have put in prior to the baby coming home. ☺

If there are multiple dogs in the family, then do each introduction individually until each dog has been introduced calmly several times over a couple of days. You can then start doing multiple dog introductions to the baby with the same rules about being calm and listening.

Remember each level of distractions we add can overstimulate the dog, so go slowly. This is why practice with the baby doll and the dog is so important: We need to have a really good idea of how this process is going to go in the weeks, or (preferably) months before the baby comes home.

Dog Trainer Tip

Let the dog say hello to all the adults in the room before saying hello to the baby. If the dog is overstimulated just saying hello to people they know, we know the introduction to a new baby is probably going to be too much for the dog. Allow the dog to leave the room, calm down and try again.

Sniff And Say Hello

Eventually you will have a dog that is on leash, calm and listening. You are ready to actually let them say hello! You have one parent sitting and the other parent (or someone else) handling the dog. You allow the dog to approach and sniff the baby.

Let the dog sniff the baby's bottom. After all, how do dogs say hello? They sniff butts! If at any point the dog gets excited or overstimulated, have the handler move the dog back and go through some commands and calm down before going back in for another hello.

Smaller dogs can be placed up on the couch or chair (if the chair has enough room for everyone). The dog is still on leash, and if the energy level spikes, remove the dog calmly from the couch and get the dog relaxed and try again. As things progress, the two parents should switch spots: One will take the baby and sit down, the other will take the leash and do the introduction the other way.

Dog Trainer Tip

If Mom has had a C-Section, then she is also going to have a lifting restriction and will not be able to handle an overexcited dog on leash. Check with the doctor on

when she will be able to complete this skill. This scenario will require a bit more planning on how and when we can switch roles.

This practice will last about 10 minutes or so and should be done 6-8 times a day until the dog is calm. Remember that with multiple dogs this will more than double your work; each dog must be calm individually and used to the introductions before then moving to multiple dog introductions. If you have three or more dogs, professional help might be a great option to help you with the beginning of the process.

Remember that we do not want to isolate the dog, so when you are not actively doing introduction practice, this is a perfect time to factor in management devices: A baby gate (my favorite tool) between the living area (where you and the baby are) and another room where the dog can be kept when not practicing. The baby gate between the two allows for separation, but the dogs are still close and can see you and start to acclimate over time. The next chapter will cover more on management devices.

Management Devices

Many folks have never had to use management devices with their dogs, so they ask, "Why do I need them now?" Let's cover why they should be used:

- As we touched on, they can allow the dog and the baby to be nearer to each other and see each other while remaining safe. This allows you to continue the normalization process even when you cannot actively be practicing. It also negates the need to isolate your pooch to the backyard (more on that later) or to a back bedroom.
- They provide a safe space for the dog when things feel scary. A fearful animal has three choices: Freeze, Flight and Fight. You want your dog to have the first two options available so that the final option is never necessary.
- There will be times when you will not be mentally capable of being alert and present. Management devices give you options to "check out" while still allowing the normalization process to continue.

Even though we are talking about our dog's management devices, think about the management devices we use with babies. If you have to cook dinner you are not going to just hope the child will be okay... *You would put the baby in a playpen so that you can pay attention to other things while knowing that the child is safely managed!*

The Big 3 Management Devices

Crate:
   This is the most common management device among dog owners. A big mistake that I frequently see as a dog trainer is when folks only put dogs in it at night and when they leave the house. When that happens, a dog's association with the crate is *I lose access to my family when I go in the crate*. *Another mistake is putting the crate in a bedroom or basement, which isolates the dog. They want to be with us, and the crate should simply be their spot in one of the main rooms where the rest of the family gathers.*

   With a baby in the picture, a crate becomes a dog's safe spot to remove themselves from stress. Now is the time to get the crate out and start getting the dog used to it again, or to teach that it is a great place.

   Some tricks for helping your dog to make a positive association with their crate: Putting toys in the crate, feeding the dog in the crate (also safer around small kids), or giving special treats a couple of times a day in the crate.

   Using the crate does require teaching children as they get older that this is an off-limits area and that they must respect the dog's space! Small hands can fit easily into a crate. You the parents must be aware and present; it is a tool, not a fix-all.

Dog Trainer Tip

When a baby is on the way I suggest removing the dog's bowl from the floor, especially in areas that the dog and baby will share. Instead of risking an incident around the food bowl, let's just take this one off the table. Get the dog used to eating in the crate, behind a baby gate or even in a separate room. This is simply the responsible thing to do.

Baby Gates:

Here's a resource that many folks forget about that can help with the normalization process, while making sure we don't isolate the dog. This allows the baby and the dog to be in close proximity but not together. This works especially well in homes with lots of doorways but can be a challenge in wide, open-concept homes where there are not a lot of doorways. There are several models available that stretch long spans, but they are often special-order items.

Again, this management device is not a fix-all or a replacement of awareness. It is merely to support the process, if it can work in your space.

Tethers

This is the most problematic of the three, but if used for specific reasons and with supervision, it can offer some limited uses. Backyard tethers are usually only about 10-20 feet long and should be attached to something sturdy. Indoors, some folks will create permanent tether locations attached to studs in the wall and others might just wrap a leash around the leg of a couch. Indoor tethers are considerably shorter, usually around 30-36 inches long. The issue is that many dogs are nervous being put on a tether; perhaps they have an owner that did not adequately normalize or socialize the use of the tether. The anxiety that a tether may work up in a dog who has a negative connotation, mixed with the introduction of a new child might incite a dog to nip or worse.

A tether should really be run by a professional dog trainer before initial use; that way there is a proper introduction, positive association and correct usage. For our purposes in this book, if your dog is not already used to a tether, adding it to the scenario of a new baby coming home is not advised.

Dog Trainer Tip

Combining one of these methods along with a playpen for the baby adds an extra layer of management, where both dog and child are in the same vicinity but not able to physically interact. If the parent's mental awareness is not quite there, then doubling up on the management devices is always preferred!

Common Issues With Dog And Baby Interactions

These are simply to make you think about your plan. If any of these hits too close to home, then the appropriate choice is to get professional help so that you will be ready.

- **Under-stimulation:** (AKA boredom) is commonly mistaken for jealousy. Don't fall for this old and tired excuse for a dog's behavior! When you bring a baby home, the dog will not get as much attention and may act out. Have you prepared your dog for less attention? Have you made sure that your dog will be getting adequate exercise (doggy daycare, walks, etc.)? Have you worn out the dog's brain with puzzle toys, classes or regular hand feeding sessions with skills practice? Don't blame the dog, just have a plan. If you don't provide your dog with entertainment, they will make their own!
- **Isolating the dog to the backyard:** This one is common for folks who are already having problems with their dogs. They get frustrated with the dog and to keep the peace and to get away from the dog, they just banish him or her to the backyard. While that sounds like a reasonable response, one or all of three things usually happen:

- The dog becomes destructive in the backyard.
- The dog becomes a barking nuisance.
- The dog becomes an escape artist.

So now you have a dog that is driving you nuts in the house, destroying your backyard, confounding your worried neighbors by roaming the neighborhood, and making all sorts of noise. Now imagine adding a new baby to this scenario. If you find yourself in this situation or think you might want to toss the dog outside, *please call a professional dog trainer and get help. Doing this before the baby comes home is the real solution!*

- **Dogs that guard stuff, or the baby:** Pick up the phone and call a trainer. Do not ever allow a possessive dog like this around a child when there are "resources" around- by this I mean food, toys or anything the dog considers to be theirs. This includes the baby- a dog could consider a baby to be a resource to guard as well! This is a complicated scenario and does not belong in a book like this. **Do not attempt this one alone.**

Dog-Baby Interaction: A Road Map

The first several years of a child's life can be hard on the family dog. Anything new to most dogs can stir up anxiety or fear. Once it becomes normal (not scary) the dog tends to relax and be okay. This process takes time but with positive reinforcement around scary things (at a safe distance) and lots of yummy treats the dog can even learn to like new things. Look at the dog's life from the day you bring the baby home to when the child is five or so....The changes are massive and fast:

1. The baby comes home. The dog thinks, "This thing is kind of noisy and it smells funny... Okay, I got this."
2. Around 3-5 months the baby starts to move (turtling and rolling over) and the dog thinks, "This is weird, and kind of scary." But after a little while the dog gets normalized, and all is okay.
3. Then the baby morphs into a toddler. The dog thinks, "Okay this thing moves fast and it's pretty terrifying." This lasts through the pulling up, wobble-walking and actually learning to walk while falling down all the time. Again, the dog eventually adjusts.

4. Then it's a 3-4-year-old child and the dog has to deal with, "This thing just took my toy! What the?!", "Oh god it's going to touch me..." and "This thing won't leave me alone!" During this time kids will pull hair, ears, tail... I have even seen kids bite the family dog!
5. Finally, the kid goes to school and the dog thinks, "Okay I guess this thing is okay, it can stay."

If you buy into the 7 for 1 rule of dogs (One year for us is 7 years for a dog) this entire process from the day you come home with the baby until they are school age (around 5 years)... Then 35 years of your dog's life has passed in constant change and stress trying to get used to this new member of the family and their developmental changes. Give your dog some grace through this process and actually understand the scope of change we are putting our fur babies through.

How Age Can Affect Behavior

Another crucial thing to consider is the age of your dog. Like humans, as dogs age their personalities, tolerances and impulse control will also change. Size can play a role too: An 8-year-old Saint Bernard is a totally different scenario than an 8-year-old Rat Terrier. Even so, dogs are individuals and there is no guarantee that Dog A and Dog B, who are both the same age, breed, gender and even size will both react the same in an identical circumstance.

Puppies (8 to 24 weeks) will have the least amount of impulse control. They will be the most energetic and hardest to predict since they have the least amount of experience.

Adolescents/Teenage Dogs (6 months to 2 years of age) tend to push back on rules and routines and not listen very well. They may even be a bit belligerent!

Adults Dogs (2 to 6 years), if well-socialized with new things, tend to be the best around all sorts of distractions, including babies and kids.

Senior Dogs (7 years and up) have every issue that older human have... Incontinence, confusion, joint pain, less flexibility to change, and even being downright grumpy at times!

Think about the following scenarios:

- A 10-week Teacup Poodle around a toddler.
- A 12-year-old German Shepherd with bad hips around an infant.
- A well socialized 5-year-old lab with a four-year-old child.

If you are concerned, call your local vet or trainer for more one-on-one help. This book is not the place to attempt a deep dive into the developmental stages of a dog's life, but rather a place to understand that it can play a role in how the dog will interact with the new baby.

Body Language And More To Consider

The following are some things to look for in a dog's body language that may signal distress- situations in which your dog is uncomfortable, stressed or anxious.

- <u>Tongue flicks and lip licking</u>: Either behavior indicates a dog's stress.
- <u>Yawning or panting</u>: It may look like your dog is just tired or hot, but in most cases, this is a dog who is uncomfortable or fearful of how the situation is going to play out.
- <u>Laid back ears</u>: This is the dog trying so very hard to tell us they are stressed.
- <u>Shaking off</u>: We have all had a dog shake water on us during or right after a bath. This would look identical to that behavior, but the dog would not be wet. This is just another way for the dog to figuratively shake off the stress of a situation.
- <u>Showing the whites of the eyes</u>: Also known as "Whale Eye", this would be the body prepping and pumping the system up for the *fight-or-flight response. With all the blood pumping, one of the last things we see is the dilation of the eyes, making the whites very pronounced.*

This is a serious warning that should not be ignored, or for that matter corrected. Back off and give the dog a chance to regroup and relax. Don't force the dog to do something they don't want to do; allow them to communicate with us.

- <u>Showing teeth or growling</u>: Showing teeth should be an easy one for folks to understand and respect, but there are still those who think it should be corrected. If the dog is scared and we punish them, how does this help their fear? I hear all the time, "I will never own a dog that growls at a child," and they relinquish, rehome or even euthanize the dog. The only thing a fearful dog can do to let us know that they are unhappy is to growl. It is the last warning that a dog can give a child. If we punish the dog for the growl, the dog might very well just bite first and ask questions later.

If you are seeing any of these behaviors, give the dog an opportunity and some space from the child to chill out. Reassure the dog. If you are still worried or my descriptions don't quite make sense, just call a trainer. That's what we're here for!

Dog Bite Statistics And The Anatomy Of A Dog Bite:

Things to consider about dog bites:

- The vast majority of dog bite victims are children under the age of 15.
- Most incidents involve a dog that the child was familiar with.
- You must continue to manage your home environment to ensure the safety of everyone in the house until your child is old enough to communicate effectively with your dog and respect his body language.
- Different life stages in dogs bring physiological changes that can affect behavior.
- The majority of the time, dog bites are due to a lack of parental management.

Let's look at an example of a stressful scenario and what can happen.

What are some things that can really stress a dog?

- Crowds
- Thunderstorms

- Children
- Not like having her head touched

Behaviors we might start to see from our dog to indicate that they are stressed:

- Yawning
- Tongue flicking
- Laid back ears

You are not paying attention, and people start petting her on top of the head. Now for the first time she growls. Suddenly a thunderstorm occurs, and she snaps at someone. Scary yes, but still not biting. One more stressor or situation that scares or affects her could push her over the edge. What if she's not feeling well (upset tummy or maybe a bad hip acting up)? The dog finally does bite. I hear about this scenario way too often, and with the owners telling me that the dog gave no warning whatsoever. With some doggy detective work, we start to see that the dog was telling people over and over, "Please leave me alone and give me a break." This is not to scare or blame anyone; it is to understand how and why things happen and how we can manage our dogs to make a very rare incident even rarer if we just pay attention. Think of it like stacking blocks (the stressors) until you build that tower past the threshold (decision to yawn, look away. lower the ears, growl, snap and finally bite) your dog just puts up with it.

If you do have a dog with a bite history and are expecting a child... Stop here and get in contact with a positive reinforcement dog trainer now.

A Final Thought

Use the time you have before the baby comes home and practice a little bit every day. Consider hiring a trainer to come in and look at the layout of your home and have them help you with where to put things. They can see possible issues that you may not have thought of. Start involving your veterinarian and your pediatrician in the process. Prepare now and you will be ready to introduce this new two-legged member of the pack!

You may feel anxious about how you are going to accomplish all of this. All it takes is investing 10-15 minutes, 2-3 times a day and you will be successful. Don't just wing it. Don't wait until 3 weeks before the baby arrives, leave stuff in boxes in the nursery, and not buy a doll. Just be consistently frequent, and frequently consistent... You are giving your dog his or her best shot to live in harmony with your newest family addition!

Good luck and remember, "Keep it Simple Stupid" and enjoy the journey!

Afterward

Well you made it, folks... The end of the book! Thanks for buying it. I really hope that you learned something in these pages that will help you communicate better with your dog. The information in these pages has come from many years of helping folks with getting the family pooch ready for the impending arrival. I promise that if you put in the time and practice with your dog (versus against your dog), you will be blown away with the progress you make.

If you enjoyed the book, there's plenty more available: We have several other books, videos (YouTube channel: Mike Deathe), an active blog, a Facebook page and other social media outlets. We love to teach folks to speak Dog as a Second Language!

While writing these books has been a pleasure, my true passion is public speaking. I love spreading the word about positive, science-based dog training. There are many people out there who don't know how simple it is to train a dog, or how enjoyable it can be! So simply Google me, Mike Deathe, or visit our business page, kissdogtraining.com, if you or your group would like to have me come give a presentation.

A final request, if you don't mind: As a small author, one of the greatest gifts that you the reader can give me is a few minutes of your time to do an online review of this book. I just need your support to get the word out. Thank you for buying the book, thank you for reading it, and thank you for being a part of training your dog the *Keep It Simple Stupid way*!

Mike

Keep It Simple Stupid (K.I.S.S.) Dog Training

www.ingramcontent.com/pod-product-compliance
Lightning Source LLC
Chambersburg PA
CBHW071222070526
44584CB00019B/3128